Creative Ideas

Creative Ideas

Ernest Holmes

Compiled by
Willis Kinnear

Science of Mind Publishing
Burbank, California

Fourteenth Printing—2004

Copyright © 1973, 2004 by Science of Mind Publishing
Foreword copyright © 2004 by Julia Cameron

Science of Mind Publishing
2600 West Magnolia Boulevard
Burbank, CA 91505

Printed in the United States of America
ISBN 0-9727184-4-3
Library of Congress Control Number: 2004112645

Design by Randall Friesen

Foreword   *xi*

Introduction   *xvi*

———

Business and Success

I Speak My Word   *2*

New Ideas and Creativity Are Mine   *4*

I Am Rich with the Richness of God   *6*

I Identify Myself with Success   *8*

I Am Supplied from the Substance of God   *10*

I Accomplish Every Good Thing   *12*

I Am Guided by the Wisdom of God   *14*

I Accept the Divine Promise   *16*

Infinite Intelligence Guides Me   *18*

I Lift Up My Cup of Acceptance   *20*

I Walk in Joy   *22*

Today Is a New Beginning   *24*

I Am Divinely Guided   *26*

My Needs Are Supplied   *28*

I Live Abundantly   *30*

Right Action and Problem Solving

I Let Go of Every Discord   *34*

I Ask in Faith and Receive   *36*

I Let Go of Restrictions   *38*

I Am Free of Problems   *40*

I Use the Law of Good   *42*

I Use My Abilities   *44*

I Discover a New Freedom   *46*

I Express My Individuality   *48*

I Act Wisely   *50*

I Am Restored and Refreshed   *52*

My Thought Is Inspired   *54*

I Accept Right Action   *56*

I Enter into a Newness of Life   *58*

I am One with Life   *60*

I See Only the Good   *62*

I Am Free of All Limitation   *64*

Health

I Accept Perfect Life   *68*

I Accept Wholeness   *70*

My Faith Is Creative   *72*

I Recognize the Spirit Within   *74*

My Heart Is Without Fear   *76*

I Surrender All Doubt   *78*

I Learn To Love   *80*

Physical Perfection Is Mine   *82*

I Forgive and Am Forgiven   *84*

I Am Radiant with Health   *86*

Divine Life Animates Me   *88*

God Lives in Me   *90*

I Find New Vitality   *92*

The Divine Flows Through Me   *94*

I Accept the Healing of Spirit   *96*

Now, Am I Made Whole   *98*

Relationships and Affairs

I Have Confidence in Life   *102*

Good Multiplies in My Experience   *104*

My Associations Are Harmonious   *106*

I See God in Everyone   *108*

I Pray Aright   *110*

Only Good Flows from Me   *112*

I Accept the Action of God   *114*

I See Good in Every Event   *116*

I Accept Divine Guidance   *118*

I Am Immersed in Perfection   *120*

I Bless What I Have   *122*

I Overcome Animosity   *124*

I Experience Satisfaction   *126*

My Relationships Are Good   *128*

I Have Great Expectations   *130*

Peace of Mind and Happiness

Living Is Worthwhile   *134*

Relaxed Living   *136*

Enlarged Horizons   *138*

A New Personality   *140*

Eliminate the Negative   *142*

Today I Live   *144*

I Am Calm and Peaceful   *146*

I Bestow the Essence of Love   *148*

I Live in Changeless Reality   *150*

My Heart Sings   *152*

I Guard My Thoughts   *154*

Love Surrounds Me   *156*

Happiness Is Mine   *158*

I Recognize My Divinity   *160*

The Gladness of Living   *162*

The Full Life   *164*

FOREWORD

Most of us know truth when we encounter it. It can be a shock—like a cold glass of water after a hike through the desert—but we usually discover we have a thirst for it. The little book you hold in your hands is pure spiritual water. It will refresh you, renew you and sustain your life. In a modern and driven world, *Creative Ideas* is a simple corrective to life gone awry. It brings calm, order and clarity to a hectic heart. It did to my own—it does still.

It was more than twenty years ago that composer

Billy May handed me a copy of these prayers. "They'll change your life," he said, with a knowing twinkle. He was absolutely right. I felt the prayers stretch and unkink my mind the way a good long walk does when you finally get out of the house. I think that spiritually, a lot of us live in the house of our own ideas, our limited thinking, and so much time indoors keeps us from enjoying the arched azure bowl of the sky—not to mention the grandeur and loftiness of our own true natures. Holmes saw all of this.

Ours remains largely a Calvinist culture. Spiritually we carry a shabby robe of self-contempt. We tell ourselves that our dreams and desires are just our "ego." We chide ourselves for dreaming, focusing on the flaws in our dreams, in our world and in ourselves. The prayers in this tiny book can change all that. They may make you—as they did me—begin to believe in a benevolent and supportive world, a world friendly to our dreams and desires, our hopes and aspirations. The prayers of Ernest Holmes are alchemical.

They convert adversity to opportunity, loss to gain, sorrow to wisdom. They are positive, affirmative and instructive. Like good medicine, they do not deny sickness but they do heal it by restoring us to health.

Ernest Holmes was—and remains—a great spiritual teacher. These small prayers carry a charge of grace. They are pocket-sized but powerful. You can read them on the subway or in the suburbs. They can start your day or lay it gently to rest. In hard times, they are calmly hopeful. In joyous times, they are gently grounding. Any challenge, difficulty or goal becomes right-sized as these prayers draw to scale the grandeur of Mind and the power of divine power to put all things right.

I have used these prayers to write books and compose music. Holmes makes The Great Creator accessible as a power within us all. I have used these prayers for comfort at times of death and as courage in times of personal challenge—physical, financial, creative. I have found them a comfort in loss and an alchemist's formula for making gold in the dross of disappointment. My book of creative recovery, *The Artist's Way*, is grounded on these bedrock principles. For me, Holmes is the modest master, the spiritual magician who transforms trouble into that magical creature, Opportunity. Holmes' optimism, like the Sacred Unicorn, is rare and real and exquisite.

Let me be clear what I mean by his "optimism." I do not find these prayers Pollyanna. They are clear-eyed and clear-headed about life's difficulties. There is no denial in them. Instead, they have an earned experience that says, "With divine help, all is always well." For Holmes this is no mere theory. It is his conviction and experience. It is the result of his Science of Mind. He has experimented with spiritual law and found it sound as well as safe. It is worth trusting, he assures us—and we ourselves are a sacred trust, waiting to be tapped.

Creative Ideas hands us the keys to the kingdom. We are wealthy and beautiful beyond our dreams. This tiny book of prayers will open your heart to its natural generosity toward life. We are each far more than we imagine, and becoming that "more" is what these small prayers will bring about.

Julia Cameron

INTRODUCTION

Today thousands are coming to believe in and use the power of affirmative prayer. We are entering into a new era of spiritual acceptance. Something definite is happening in the field of spiritual thought and endeavor. From all sources we are coming to realize that affirmative prayer is dynamic. It should be easier today than ever before for people to accept the simple teaching that there is a power greater than we are which desires our good, and a law of good which we may consciously use for definite purposes.

We shall be both inspirational and scientific when we come to believe this—inspirational in the belief and scientific in the use of the law. Fundamental to every science is the use of law. This is equally true in the science of Mind, for we are not dealing with chaotic laws that may or may not respond to us; we are dealing with the certainty of a reaction which is equal to the action, or a response that is equal to our own conviction. We are dealing with a definite principle, but the conviction is personal, a thing of warmth, of color and feeling.

Spiritual mind treatment is an affirmation of the divine presence in and through all things, all people, and all events. God is one as the divine presence and the intelligent law governing all things. We live in this divine presence and may consciously use this universal law.

We should use it definitely and consciously, and we should reach a place where our belief transcends the need for having faith because it already incorporates the essence of faith by the very fact of its complete acceptance.

But someone might ask: "How does our prayer, our treatment, or our affirmation reach the person, the place, or the thing we wish to help?" This question both simplifies and answers itself when we come to realize that there is but one Spirit, one Mind, and one law, and that we all are identified in this one life, not as being separate from it but as individualized expressions of it. Since this is true, whenever we identify our thinking with some person, place, or thing, we identify that person, place, or thing as the object of that thinking, and automatically, because there is but one law or intelligence operating, the result of that thinking will be for that person, place, or thing. Since the person, place, or thing we are treating, or praying for as some term it, is in the one Spirit, the one Mind, and the one law, then the mere act of identifying that person, place, or thing with our affirmation causes the reaction of that affirmation to appear.

We must come not only to believe and accept, but also permanently to know that there is a power greater than we are, and we can use it. Then as we affirm that we are one with the living Spirit, that God is all there is and there is nothing else, our word, being the presence and the power and the activity of that Spirit, is the law of good and cannot fail to operate. Let us feel that there is something permanent about the word we have spoken. Just as we plant a seed and walk away from it, nature takes it up, and the law of its own being evolves it, so let us believe the same thing about our word—something takes it up, something evolves it, and something will make it manifest in our experience.

Ernest Holmes

You set a goal above all goals and yet

Fulfillment of the goal that God has set

That all should find themselves, grow and expand

Until they are to God another hand,

Another eye, to see and bring to birth

New forms of beauty chiseled here on earth.

Business and Success

I SPEAK MY WORD

...he is in one mind, and who can turn him?....

JOB 23:13

Emerson tells us that "there is one mind common to all individual men." It is this eternal mind which we use. The Mind of God must be peace, joy, and perfection. We enter into this divine state of being in such degree as our thoughts are peaceful, joyous, and perfect. To practice the presence of God is to think in terms of perfection and wholeness, and results in the fulfillment of every right desire.

We live in Mind and our thoughts go out into Mind to be fulfilled. This is the principle of spiritual mind treatment and demonstration. Each one individualizes this universal Mind in a unique and personal way. This is our divine inheritance. But we have drawn too lightly upon it, not fully realizing as Jesus did the significance of our relationship with the Infinite.

Today I learn to enter more fully into my divine companionship. I speak my word of good, knowing that it will not return unto me void because it bears the peace and joy and perfection that is of God.

I rightly accomplish and prosper as I persistently keep my desires in accord with God's nature.

NEW IDEAS AND
CREATIVITY ARE MINE

...The Son can do nothing of himself....

JOHN 5:19

Since God is all there is—the only presence, the only power, and the only mind or intelligence—when we conceive a new idea, we are thinking directly from the creativity of God. It is not our isolated, limited human personality that projects this new idea. We are merely the instrument through which this projection takes place. God is the only creator, there is nothing else besides. God is both the inventor of a game and those who play it, the author and the actor, the song and the singer.

Out of the limitless creativity of God, I accept the flow of new

4

ideas. My whole consciousness is alive, awake, and aware to them. I am impregnated with new ideas, and they shall bear fruit according to the divine pattern contained within them.

Today I expect new ways of doing things. I expect everything in my experience to enlarge, deepen, and broaden. I expect more good, more enthusiasm, more accomplishment than ever before. There now opens up before me a world of new ideas, new thoughts, new people, and new situations.

Today is a new beginning. The divine influx now makes this day expansive and expressive of the creative source of all things.

I AM RICH WITH
THE RICHNESS OF GOD

※

...the world is mine, and the fullness thereof.

PSALM 50:12

The Divine will never fail us if we have implicit faith in It. But we are so caught with fear and doubt and uncertainty that it becomes necessary for us to take time every day to reaffirm our union with the great out-flowing givingness of life. This is the purpose of meditation and prayer.

It is natural that we should wish the abundant life. It is right that we should expect it. God has already made the gift; it is up to us to accept it.

Today I accept God's gift of abundance. Today everything that I am and have is increased by it. I identify everything I do with success. I think affirmatively, and in all my prayers I accept abundance. Whatever I need, whenever I need it, wherever I need it, for as long as I need it, will always be at hand.

I no longer see negation or delay or stagnation in my undertakings but, rather, claim that the action of the living Spirit prospers everything I do, increases every good I possess, and brings success to me and everyone I meet.

Everything I think about and do is animated by the divine presence, sustained by the infinite power, and multiplied by the divine goodness.

I IDENTIFY MYSELF
WITH SUCCESS

...he shall give thee the desires of thine heart.

PSALM 37:4

It is impossible to be successful while you identify yourself with failure. You tend to attract to yourself circumstances and situations which are like the images of your thought.

Knowing this, realize that if you would change undesirable objective business experiences, you must first reverse their subjective patterns in your thought. When you see you have patterns of thought that have identified you with lack of success or failure, you must definitely and specifically replace them with ideas and statements affirming the success you desire.

I know that I am in partnership with the infinite. I identify myself with this partnership knowing that it always leads to success. I accept that the action of infinite intelligence is back of everything. It is always manifesting itself, and it now does so through the thought pattern of success I am establishing for myself.

Conditions and situations about me now start to correspond to my new ideas about them. The invisible presence and power indwelling and surrounding me, which is forever making manifest my thought, now creates for me the success with which I have identified my thought.

I AM SUPPLIED FROM
THE SUBSTANCE OF GOD

The Father...hath given all things....
JOHN 3:35

We all have need of many things. We cannot believe that the divine Spirit wishes to withhold any good from us. It is the nature of God to give, and it is our nature to receive.

Back of every idea of supply, every need in our human lives, there is something which forever more gives of itself and takes the form of our experiences when we permit it to. Whether it be a house to live in, money that we have need of, or employment that furnishes the gratification of adequate self-expression, always there is the giver flowing into these things. But God cannot give if we refuse to accept.

Today I live in the quiet, joyous expectation of good. God is not only my life, It is also the substance taking form in my experience. God is not only the actor, but It is acting through me now. God is not only the giver, It is also the gift.

This gift I receive in joy, with gratitude, and with a complete sense of security. I expect everything I do to prosper and new and wonderful experiences to come to me. I now live in complete confidence that the realm of heaven is here and now and that I experience it now. I am prospered in everything I do.

I ACCOMPLISH
EVERY GOOD THING

...the same God which worketh all in all.

I CORINTHIANS 12:6

We are all engaged in different activities which express our unique individualization. But it is the same God working in all of us—one power is working, one life is expressing, one energy is animating, one presence flowing through, and one law controlling each of us.

The one Mind is working in and through us now as spontaneous expression. Back of our smallest act is the strength of the universe. Behind our thoughts is the infinite thinker. Diffused through our every activity is the divine presence.

Today I affirm that all my thoughts are formulated in the divine Mind; all of my actions are sustained by the infinite energy; all the power there is and all the presence there is is right where I am. I now open the channels of my thought to the influx of this divine presence which is doing something unique and different through me. I sense its impact on my thought and imagination. I see it operating through all my actions. There is that within me which doeth all things well. As I now surrender myself completely to that one power, that one all-knowing Mind, that one presence, I become a channel for Its successful expression and achievement.

I AM GUIDED BY
THE WISDOM OF GOD

If any of you lack wisdom, let him ask of God....
JAMES 1:5

A universal and infinite intelligence governs everything, holds everything in its place, and directs the
course of everything. The intelligence that governs the
planets in their courses is the same intelligence that is
manifesting in the mind of humankind. The personal
use we make of it to direct and govern our activities
depends upon our personal choice.

*Today I am guided by the wisdom of God in everything I
think, say, or do. Since there is nothing large or small to the
infinite, there is nothing in my experience beyond its action. I
affirm the presence of this wisdom and accept and acknowledge*

its action in my every endeavor. I permit it to guide me in every circumstance.

In this knowledge, I now know how to plan my life and direct my path because God is doing this for me by doing it through me. There is no uncertainty or confusion. The divine Spirit always knows what to do and how to do it, so I am never without guidance in the successful achievement of my good desires. My every thought, act, and purpose is guided by this wisdom.

I ACCEPT THE
DIVINE PROMISE

🌾

The Lord is not slack concerning his promise....

II PETER 3:9

The Bible is filled with divine promises, revealed through the spiritual intuition of great souls. We are promised long life and happiness, riches and abundance, health and success. More particularly, we are told that these promises are fulfilled right now, in the day in which we live. We need not wait, but only need to accept them now.

This acceptance is a mental as well as a spiritual act. The mind needs to accept its highest hope in complete confidence, placing its entire reliance on a power greater than itself.

Today I accept with joy and gratitude the divine promises of riches, abundance, and success. I accept the enveloping presence that sustains me as now manifesting in my experience a greater supply of all those things which make living a greater joy. My increased good deprives no one, for God's good knows no limitation.

I now know that as God's creativity flows in and through me into complete expression, I experience a good beyond my fondest imagination, beyond my greatest dream. I am given to even more abundantly than I ask, for the promises of God are as certain as life, as immutable as law, as personal as my heart-beat. And so it is.

INFINITE INTELLIGENCE
GUIDES ME

🦋

...they seek me daily, and delight to know my ways....
ISAIAH 58:2

God is all there is, and in every action and reaction, in every circumstance and situation,
whether we call it big or little, there is one power governing, and only one. Science, logic, mathematics, reason, and revelation are on the side of the one who
proclaims the allness of God.

Feeling and thinking and sensing this allness, we
enter into conscious communion with it; and in some
subtle way, which we do not understand, its essence
flows out into our act, spilling itself in and through
everything we do, bringing to bear upon the simplest
problems of life an intelligence greater than the

human and a power that is transcendent.

Today I affirm the supremacy of good, and everything within me responds to it and announces its presence. A power greater than I am flows through me into everything I do or think about, automatically making everything whole.

There is a transcendence coordinating, unifying, causing all the experiences of my life to blend into its unity, into its oneness, and proclaiming the power of its might. I now accept the successful action of the divine governor in everything I do and the abundant expression of the divine provider fulfilling all my needs.

I LIFT UP MY
CUP OF ACCEPTANCE

✼

And God is able to make all grace abound toward you....
II CORINTHIANS 9:8

We lift up our cup of acceptance to the divine bounty when we think affirmatively and give thanks to the giver of all life. Daily we should practice affirming that our cup is filled and running over, always remembering that what we affirm for ourselves we must affirm for others. Living and letting live, giving and receiving, loving and being loved, our experience is filled with God's abundance.

I am living in the continual expectancy that every good thing in my experience shall be multiplied. There is neither doubt nor uncertainty in my mind. I know that the Spirit of God has made me, and the breath of the Almighty has given me life. I have complete confidence in this Spirit and Its action in my experience.

I affirm that today is filled with blessing for myself and others. The past is gone, and I gladly release it and let it go. The present is filled with peace and joy and the future with hope. Gratefully I accept of the divine love and givingness and extend them to everyone I meet. I am made whole with the wholeness of the Spirit.

I am guided into right action and successful accomplishment of all my good desires. This I accept. This I experience.

I WALK
IN JOY

※

He shall call upon me, and I will answer him....
PSALM 91:15

We should not consider that our good is something that is to transpire in the future, but rather that it is transpiring right now, today, in the present moment in which we live. We need to recognize that the good we desire can become ours only as we accept it now.

Every good thing necessary to my success already belongs to the realm of God, which I know is at hand. So today I am expecting good to happen to me. I anticipate success in all my activities. I believe that divine intelligence guides me in all my right activities; and because I know that God always succeeds,

It now succeeds in and through my endeavors. I know that now everything necessary to my success is being brought about, and there is complete fulfillment of every worthwhile idea.

I accept that God is active in my affairs. Knowing that God is in all people, there is joyous cooperation with others. Therefore I help and am helped. Knowing that God is the great giver, I accept God's gift and myself become a giver to life. The abundance of God that contains all that belongs to my life of good is available to me today. I accept it now, and it manifests in and through me, and I am prospered.

TODAY IS A
NEW BEGINNING

※

…I create new heavens and a new earth….
Isaiah 65:17

Nothing is ever twice alike. Everything is continuously being re-created, and it literally is true that the creative Spirit is forever making all things new. We must permit It to make them new for us.

I live today as though the words of this my affirmative prayer were already accomplished facts in my experience. I empty my mind of every fear and doubt. I condemn no one and no thing, not even myself. I forget that which is past and have no fear of the future.

I live in harmony with people and with all situations that surround me. I see and feel the presence of good running through everything. I have complete faith that this divine presence reveals itself to me in my every thought, every word, and every act.

There is nothing in my thought about the past or the future that can in any way deny me the pleasure and privilege of living today as though everything was complete and perfect. My whole expectancy is of much and more, of good and better.

The future is bright with hope and fulfillment. The present is perfect, and no past failure mars today's understanding. Today is the start of my new and more successful experience of achievement. And so it is.

I AM
DIVINELY GUIDED

❧

…let me speak, and answer thou me.

JOB 13:22

We believe that the Mind of God governs all things. We believe that there is a divine intelligence governing and guiding, counseling and advising, causing us to know what to do under every circumstance and at all times, if we will but trust it.

Our mind is the Mind of God within us. God has no problems, for God is the presence and the power that knows all things and can do all things. If we but take our problem to that high place in our consciousness, it will disappear as we feel the answer is taking the place of the problem. There is nothing that can keep this from happening except our own thought of doubt or limitation.

Today I do affirm that I am divinely guided and that the Spirit goes before me and paves the way. There is that within which knows what to do and how to do it, and it compels me to act on what it knows.

I accept this guidance as now flowing forth into action through me. Therefore I shall do that which I should do, I shall know that which I need to know, I shall encounter those new ideas I need. With nonresistance and complete acceptance, I let the inward stream of life carry me safely and surely to the accomplishment of my every good purpose.

MY NEEDS
ARE SUPPLIED

Every good gift…cometh down from the Father….
JAMES 1:17

The science of spiritual mind treatment cannot promise something for nothing. It does, however, teach, and it can demonstrate, that a betterment of circumstances and conditions can be brought about through the realization that there is active in our undertakings a power greater than we are.

It would be unthinkable to believe that the creative intelligence of the universe could lack anything, or that it could plan for its creation to lack that which expresses its own being. The Divine could only intend good and abundance for Its creation, and we need to know that Its nature is forever flowing into everything we do.

As I desire to do only that which is good and constructive, life-giving and life-expressing, the divine abundance forever manifests in my endeavors. Therefore I know that I shall prosper in everything I do. I know that I exist in a limitless possibility and that the infinite good is right where I am and active in my experience.

I believe that everything for complete self-expression is now the law of my being. New thoughts, new ideas, new situations now unfold before me. There are new opportunities for achievement and abundant living. This I accept, and this I expect.

I LIVE
ABUNDANTLY

Thou…satisfiest the desire of every living thing.
PSALM 145:16

Why should we go through life as though it were something that had to be endured; as if there were not enough joy, happiness, and good to go around? We always seem to be limiting the possibility of experiencing the good things of life.

If we really are in union with a divine source, then we should have a feeling of abundance in everything we do, for our source contains all things, whether we call them big or little. We need to feel that the Divine is surging forth into everything we do, that infinite intelligence is flowing into our consciousness, and that the creativity of the universe is centered in our act and motivating it.

Should we properly attune our consciousness to this divine abundance, automatically we would find betterment in everything we do, a broader and deeper experience, a higher realization, and a greater good.

Today I expect the more abundant life. I keep my thought open to new experiences and opportunities for greater self-expression. As I share and give of myself to life, the one life pours its bounty upon me. As God finds a fuller outlet through me, I experience a new consciousness of joy, peace, and security.

The boon you ask of life,
This greater good
Is open unto all, but life will give
A love to all who know
how to receive;
It mirrors back in form
what you expect.
This is the circle of life
and this its story.
Earth is but mirror of a greater glory.

Right Action and Problem Solving

I LET GO OF
EVERY DISCORD

✤

…whereas I was blind, now I see.
JOHN 9:25

There is that within us which is completely conscious of its unity with good, of its oneness with
all the power there is, and all the presence there is, and
all the life there is. Upon this power, presence, and life
we should depend with implicit certainty, with complete confidence, and with absolute assurance.

We need to know that as we accept its action, it has
the power to overcome every discord in our experience and wipe out every sense of fear or confusion. As
we affirm and believe that nothing can oppose the
action of God, and come to accept that action in our
life, everything unlike Its good is overcome.

I now permit the Spirit within me to express Itself in freedom, bringing increased joy and harmony into my experience. I allow the divine wholeness to flow through me into ever-widening fields of activity bringing peace where there was confusion, joy where there was discord. Order, the law of God, reigns supreme in my life.

I silence my turbulent thoughts and direct my attention to the acceptance of God's perfect action in my experience. As I do so, all power is delivered unto me, and this I use for my own and everyone's good.

I ASK IN FAITH
AND RECEIVE

ask, and ye shall receive....
John 16:24

This is one of the most wonderful statements ever uttered. It implies that there is a power which can and will honor your request. But it is only as you let go of the lesser that you can take hold of the greater, only as you drop confusion that you can entertain peace, only as you transcend doubt and fear that you can be lifted up to the hilltops of the inner life.

In asking, you must identify yourself with the greatness of Spirit. Permit your consciousness, through faith, to rise to a greater and broader realization of that divine presence which is always delivering itself to you.

Through an awareness of the immediate presence and action of Spirit, I learn to look quietly and calmly upon every negative situation, seeing through it to the other side, to the invisible reality which molds conditions and re-creates them after a more nearly perfect pattern.

I know that through the action of law, my word transmutes every energy into constructive action, producing harmony, success, and right action in my experience. I know that in this consciousness of reality rests the supply for my every need. As I now accept, I receive.

I LET GO OF
RESTRICTIONS

...If God be for us, who can be against us?
ROMANS 8:31

Realizing that all action starts in, and is a result of, consciousness, prepare your mind to receive the best that life has to offer. Become increasingly aware of the presence, the one life, and the one Spirit, which is God. The Spirit works through you according to your belief.

So drop all sense of lack or limitation from thought. All things are possible to the Spirit, therefore everything is possible to you in such degree as you believe in and accept the operation of Spirit in life. And there is that within you which is aware of its oneness with power, of its unity with life.

I now allow the divine wholeness to flow through me in ever-widening circles of activity. Every sense of limitation melts away, and every good I have experienced is now increased. Every joy that has come into my life is multiplied, and there is a new influx of inspiration into my thought. I see more clearly than ever before that my divine birthright is freedom, joy, and the experience of good.

The Divine is not limited, so as a creation of the Divine, I let go of all restricting ideas. Knowing that life gives according to my faith, I lift my thought, I elevate my faith. I accept the divine presence as now bountifully expressing as peace and harmony in my life.

I AM FREE
OF PROBLEMS

*

Thou madest him to have dominion....
PSALM 8:6

There is a power operating through, a presence inspiring, an intelligence guiding, and a law of good sustaining you. Upon this presence, this power, and this law, you may place complete reliance.

Because you live in this divine presence, and because it is in you, you may know that the creative law of good, which is infinite and which has all power, can do for you or bring to you anything and everything necessary to your complete happiness and the solving of your every difficulty. Its whole and only desire for you is one of freedom and joy.

I know that freedom from problems, whatever they may be, and a new joy are mine today. This freedom and joy spontaneously express themselves in my experience. There is nothing in me that can obstruct their passage. I permit them to flow through me in all their wonder and might.

I am conscious of an infinite wisdom directing me. Whatever I ought to know, I shall know; whatever I ought to do, I shall do. My every thought and decision is molded by infinite Mind and expressed through law into my experience. My problems and difficulties are dissolved and melt away as I now declare that the action of intelligence makes all things right in my life.

I USE THE
LAW OF GOOD

✤

…I delight in the law of God….
ROMANS 7:22

All creation is a manifestation of the delight of God—God seeing Itself in form, experiencing Itself in Its own actions, and knowing Itself in us as us. For the highest God and the innermost God is one God, and not two. Although God is what we are, we are at the same time subject to Its exact law that governs everything. Let us then learn to recognize ourselves as creations of God and find delight in using the law of God to enhance Its expression through us as what we are.

I am one with the infinite Spirit of love, one with the out-

pouring of the divine life. I am governed by the perfect law of the inward man, made in the image and likeness of that which is pure, whole, and perfect.

I know that the law of good is absolute; it is complete; it is operating in and through me now, bringing about everything that is good, everything that is right.

Since this law must be perfect as well as exact, and since it must know how to bring everything about that is necessary to my good, I place my whole trust in it. And so today and every day, I accept the perfect action of the law of good as governing and making all things right in my world.

I USE MY
ABILITIES

...there is no power but of God....
ROMANS 13:1

The secret of affirmative prayer lies in the realization that there is a power of good in the universe greater than we are and that we can use it. All scientists know that they take power out of life; they do not put it in. And so it is in dealing with that more subtle energy and power which we call Mind, or Spirit.

One of the first things to do is to learn to accept and to expect this power to flow through everything we do. We must combine our belief in this power with the conscious use of it for definite purposes. We have greater ability and resources than we have yet realized.

Believing that there is an infinite power in the universe, a power of good greater than I am, I now accept its action in my life. I know that there is a strength and a vitality, a livingness flowing through me out into everything I think, or say, or do.

I am the very embodiment of this power, its energy and action. There is no sense of weakness or lack of strength; rather, the fullness and the perfection of this power is always present, always active. I completely recognize and accept the flow of this power through me, manifesting itself in right ways in every aspect of my life.

I DISCOVER A
NEW FREEDOM

…Ye must be born again.
JOHN 3:7

By far the larger part of our thinking processes are automatic, casting, as it were, the images of their acceptance into the universal Mind which reacts upon them. And thus it is that fear can bring about the condition feared while faith can reverse it.

In spiritual mind treatment, affirmation and denial are for the purpose of erasing wrong thought patterns and establishing correct ones. Affirmation can either instantly or gradually establish an inward recognition which becomes permanent. The Mind principle is like a mirror reflecting the conscious declarations of the good we desire.

Today I affirm the action of God in my life, and I deny that there is any presence or power of real evil in the universe. I affirm the presence of love and repudiate every belief that hate has any power. I affirm that peace exists in my experience and deny confusion. I affirm joy and declare that sadness has no place in my consciousness. I affirm that God is over all, in all, and through all.

There is nothing out of the past that can limit me, and there is nothing in me that can limit my future. I experience a new freedom and joy in living.

I EXPRESS MY
INDIVIDUALITY

…diversities of gifts, but the same Spirit.

I Corinthians 12:4

It is right and necessary that we should be individuals. The divine Spirit never made any two things alike—no two rosebushes, two snowflakes, two grains of sand, or two persons. We are all just a little unique, for each wears a different face; but behind each is the one presence—God.

Unity does not mean uniformity. Unity means that everything draws its strength, its power, and its ability to live from the one source. One life does flow through everything, but it is never monotonous; it is forever doing new things in and through each of us.

I affirm that the original Spirit is doing something new through me today. Therefore everything I do is original; it is a new creation. There is a new enthusiasm, a new zest for living.

The divine Spirit is flowing through me in an individual way, and I accept the genius of my own being. All the presence there is, is flowing through me in an original manner. I accept its right action, its new ideas. I continually invite the inspiration, the illumination, and the guidance of God which I recognize. As I cooperate with them, I express my divine individuality and experience more of my limitless potentiality.

I ACT
WISELY

...believe that ye receive....

MARK 11:24

There could be no more explicit instruction for effective prayer than is contained in these words of Jesus. We actually are to believe that we already possess the object of our desire when we ask for it. We are to accept it even as we believe in the harvest which follows the spring planting. Therefore, every planting should be one of hope and every harvest one of fulfillment. We must learn to accept the good we desire and affirm its presence in our experience.

Realizing that there is a law of good that governs my experience, I lose every thought of doubt, fear, or uncertainty and accept the good I desire, here and now.

Realizing that this law of God not only knows how to create, but must contain within itself all the details of its own creation, I let go of every thought of outlining and accept the perfect answer today. And because there is no sense of strain in this, I relax in quiet contentment, while at the same time realizing that what the law does for me, it must do through me.

I declare that I not only know what to do, but am impelled to act, to move objectively. I move into a greater sphere of action and life with certainty, calm confidence, and limitless trust.

I AM RESTORED
AND REFRESHED

The Lord is my shepherd…He restoreth my soul.…
PSALM 23:1, 3

When we consider the thought that the Lord is our shepherd, we come to feel that we are one with the divine presence and enter into a conscious communion with it. This is spiritual meditation and affirmative prayer. It is through spiritual meditation that we reach out, or in, to that divine presence which has its indwelling place in the sanctuary of our own heart, and is also everywhere. When we believe this and know that God can sustain us as well as restore us, then our only need is to accept such divine action.

I now lay aside every doubt or fear and gladly enter into a newness of life. I do believe that the Lord is my shepherd. I do believe that the Lord restoreth my soul.

I am now aware that the divine presence is not only close to me, it is not only where I am, it is also within me and what I am; therefore I know that not only shall I not want, but my cup shall run over. I am sustained by an infinite power, guided by an infinite intelligence, guarded by an infinite love.

There is a power greater than I am on which I now rely, and I let this intelligence govern and guide and protect me in all my ways. Nothing can oppose God's right action in my life.

MY THOUGHT
IS INSPIRED

And the Lord, he it is that doth go before thee....
DEUTERONOMY 31:8

We should believe that God is the invisible partner in our lives and affirm that divine love goes before us and prepares the way. We should permit ourselves to be guided, for there is something within us, deep at the center of our being, which knows what we ought to do and how we ought to do it. If we listen to the divine presence, it will direct us and guide us. Right thoughts and ideas will come to us, and we will be compelled to express them in our experience.

I know how to meet every situation in calm trust and with the complete conviction that divine intelligence is guiding me. I am always impelled into right action.

I wish to do only that which is constructive and life-giving; therefore I know that everything I do is prospered. Everything I touch is quickened into a newness of life and action. Every constructive purpose in my life is fulfilled. I have a deep sense of inner calm, a complete assurance that all is well.

The same intelligence that guides the earth around the sun is now acting as the law of good in my personal experience. I do accept divine guidance and thank God for the inspiration, joy, and harmony that are now being established as my experience.

I ACCEPT
RIGHT ACTION

※

As for God, his way is perfect....
PSALM 18:30

To be effective, prayer must be affirmative; but it is not enough merely to affirm the presence of God. We must add to this realization the thought that divine intelligence is acting in and through us now. Prayer is not wishful or wistful thinking, nor is it an escape from objective reality. To get lost in our prayers might give us an unconscious desire to escape from the activities of life. Therefore we affirm that divine intelligence not only knows what to do, but also impels us to act on its knowing.

I hand my life, my affairs, and my problems over to divine intelligence, to the power that knows how to do everything. I do this in the complete conviction that I receive only good and right action into my experience.

I know there is nothing in me that can doubt either the divine goodness or the operation of its law in my life. I believe that everything necessary to the fulfillment of my every good desire is now in full operation, that all the circumstances in my life are tending to rightly bring them about. Whatever I need to do, I am impelled to do knowing I am intelligently guided.

I accept the new good that now comes into my life.

I ENTER INTO A
NEWNESS OF LIFE

Commit thy way unto the Lord....
PSALM 37:5

Sometimes we are confronted with problems which we do not seem able to solve, and now is the time to prove to ourselves that there is an intelligence which knows how to bring the right things to pass for us.

In doing this, we should shut everything else out of our minds and rest quietly for a few minutes while we confidently affirm the divine presence and actually believe that it is guiding us. Now think of your problem and consciously take it into your thought, not as a problem, but as though you were receiving the answer. Then affirm the following:

I believe that divine intelligence, which is the Mind of God, is guiding and directing my thoughts and acts. I believe that God already knows the answer to this particular problem; therefore I let go of it and listen to the answer. The answer to this problem exists in the Mind of God and is revealed to my mind now. Something in me knows what to do. I joyfully accept its guidance.

I am now open to new ideas, new hopes, and new aspirations. This which recently seemed a problem no longer exists, for the Mind of God which knows the answer is quietly flowing through my thought and feeling. I accept the answer from the giver of all life.

I AM ONE
WITH LIFE

🦟

God is a Spirit…worship him in spirit and in truth.
JOHN 4:24

There is one God, and out of this oneness proceeds all that really is. Wonderful indeed is this conception of the union of all life which Jesus proclaimed: "I and my Father are one." All cause and all effect proceed from the invisible Spirit.

Each person is one with this Spirit and cannot be separated from It. Our word has power because our word is the action of God through our thought. This power is; we use it, we do not have to create it. Let us seek to use the divine nature more generously with a greater idea of God's beneficence and abundance available to us.

Regardless of what my problem may be, or in what direction I need guidance, I know that today I walk in a full understanding of my oneness with God. God is at the center of my being, and from this center I receive inspiration which governs my every thought and every act with certainty, love, and peace.

My guidance is assured as I accept the all-knowing creative action of God through what I am. I know exactly what to do and how to do it for the establishing of right action for myself and all concerned in my life. God has no problems, and as I am an expression and creation of God, all difficulties are now removed from my experience.

I SEE ONLY
THE GOOD

He brought them out of darkness....
PSALM 107:14

To be free from the bondage of fear, superstition, and anxiety, the mind must be riveted on freedom; the thought must rise transcendent over the bondage. If we do this, then we are brought out of the shadow of darkness into the light of the glorious freedom of the children of God that we are. If we would be free, the mind and heart must be open to the influx of divine intelligence. It is only from such spiritual enlightenment that we can gain the freedom we seek.

Today I am resolved to see only the good—God. Whatever there is in my thought that is unlike this and has kept me in bondage is wiped away. A new spiritual enlightenment floods my mind as I become aware of the divine presence as peace, joy, and harmony at the center of my being.

Whatever there is in my thought or experience that has barred me from a fuller experience of the good life is now resolved and dissolved. I accept the constructive, affirmative, creative action of God, which is boundless and free, as now making me free of all limitation.

I think only of good; my experience is filled only with good. My acceptance of the good of God as an actuality in my life now transcends all unlike it and makes my life new.

I AM FREE OF
ALL LIMITATION

…uphold me with thy free spirit.
PSALM 51:12

Divine intelligence produces everything, nourishes everything, and maintains everything. It spreads itself over everything; it flows through everything and is in all things. Indeed, being all that is, there can be nothing outside it. So in such degree as we understand God, we become liberated. We need to recognize the divine in everything; to see it everywhere.

There is a mystical presence which pervades the universe. It is always welling up in our consciousness, evermore proclaiming itself as the source of all. The Bible says that there is "One God and Father of all, who is above all, and through all, and in you all."

I know that that which I am is God in me, as me. In this knowledge, I know that my spirit is free of all limitations. I know that my mind knows this truth about myself. My thoughts now affirm my divine source. My thoughts are free of ideas of limitation, and they cease hindering the outflow of the indwelling presence.

As I now know and declare the truth of my real nature, there becomes manifest in my thinking and experience the perfection and wholeness of God which rightfully belong to me. I am free with the freedom of God, and all things in my life are good.

Without
PEACE there
is no happiness

Without
HAPPINESS there
can be no enthusiasm

Without
ENTHUSIASM
there can be no
JOY IN
LIFE

Health

I ACCEPT
PERFECT LIFE

...the prayer of faith shall save the sick....
JAMES 5:15

When we say that our body is spiritual, we are not denying our physical body. The physical is included within the spiritual. If the Spirit, or divine intelligence, has seen fit to give us a physical body, it would be absurd to think of our body as an illusion unworthy of our attention. Rather, we should think of it as a spiritual instrument, and every statement we make about it or belief we hold about it which accepts spiritual perfection as the substance of the body, tends to heal.

My body is the temple of the living Spirit. It is spiritual sub-

stance now. Every part of my body is in harmony with the living Spirit within me. The life of this Spirit flows through every atom of my being, vitalizing, invigorating, and renewing every part of my physical body.

There is a pattern of perfection at the center of my being which is now operating through every organ, function, action, and reaction. My body is forever renewed by the Spirit, and I am now made vigorous and whole.

The life of the Spirit is my life, and its strength is my strength. I am born of the Spirit. I am in the Spirit. I am the Spirit made manifest.

I ACCEPT
WHOLENESS

🌿

…thy faith hath made thee whole.

MATTHEW 9:22

Let us see if we cannot let our faith soar and go into the mountain of the Lord, which is the secret place of the most high within us, and let the whole harmony of our lives flow from that perfect Spirit which is at the center of everything. Through a conscious acceptance of the fullness of the presence of God, there flows in and through us a joy, a love, and a wholeness that touches every part of our being.

I am one with the infinite and perfect Spirit, the giver of all good and perfect gifts. I open my mind and my heart and, indeed, my body to the inflow of this divine presence. I know that this living presence is in every cell of my body and every function of my being. I accept it as my health of body, here and now. I accept it as that which takes from me all that is unlike the perfect expression of life.

There is no doubt or fear in my mind that rejects in any way all that God is, right here and right now. And I decree that all I now bring into the scope of my thought is blessed and healed through the presence of good which is within.

I drink at the fount of life and am made whole.

MY FAITH
IS CREATIVE

...decree a thing, and it shall be established unto thee....
JOB 22:28

Faith acts like a law, because it is a law. It is the law of Mind in action. When we realize this, we no longer feel that we must have faith in ourselves as isolated beings; but rather, that as human beings, we are included in the great law of life.

Then we can rest in complete confidence that our words, spoken in faith, are the presence and power and activity of the Spirit in us. All sense of making things happen or holding thoughts or concentrating is put aside, and with childlike acceptance, we make known our requests with thanksgiving.

I am one with God. Nothing can separate me from the Spirit within. With complete faith in Its presence and power, I know that all that I am and do is the divine presence expressing itself through me.

I now speak my word of health for my body, my feelings, and my thoughts, knowing that the Spirit within is the power which brings this wholeness into complete being. I speak the word of joy, and the Spirit within frees me from loneliness and sadness. The thoughts I think and the words I speak are brought to pass because it is God speaking them through me.

I RECOGNIZE
THE SPIRIT WITHIN

…ye are God's building.
I CORINTHIANS 3:9

Spiritual mind healing has long since passed the experimental stage. We now know that we cannot tell where the body begins and the mind leaves off, and many of us believe that the organs, actions, and functions of the physical body are activities of infinite intelligence within us. To come to realize, then, that there is one body, which is the body of God, and which at the same time is our own body, is to accept a greater influx of the one life. We should daily affirm:

There is one life, that life is God, that life is my life now. Every organ, action, and function of my physical body is in harmony with the divine life. There is perfect assimilation, perfect circulation, and perfect elimination.

If there is anything in me that does not belong, it is removed. If there is anything that my physical being needs that it does not appear to have, it is supplied. My body is daily renewed after that image of perfection of it which is held in the Mind of God.

I affirm, then, that my body is the body of God; the life of the Spirit does circulate through it, the law of the Spirit does govern it, the love of the Spirit does sustain it. My whole life is God in action.

MY HEART IS
WITHOUT FEAR

…my heart shall not fear.…
PSALM 27:3

Fear is the only thing we need be afraid of. It is neither the host camped against us nor the confusion around us that we need to fear; it is a lack of confidence in the good that alone should cause concern. We know that right finally resolves everything opposed to it.

In confidence, then, and with a calm sense of peace, we know that the truth never fails to win every issue. The power of good is with us. The power of the Spirit is supreme over every antagonist. We should cherish no fear, for when we neither fear nor hate, we come to understand the unity of life. The nature of God cannot be other than that of peace and love.

I know that God is within me, and I know that this divine Spirit is perfect. I enter into Its peace and love and am secure with a sense of Its protection. Today my heart is without fear. I have implicit confidence in God's action through me, guiding and directing me. The power of the infinite sustains and upholds me.

I enter into a conscious union with the Spirit, and my heart is without fear, for the unerring judgment of divine intelligence directs my faith and makes plain the way before me. I enter this day with joy and look to tomorrow with courage and confidence.

I SURRENDER
ALL DOUBT

...to be spiritually minded is life and peace.
ROMANS 8:6

We should always keep in mind that we are beneficiaries of life. We do not put the chicken in the egg or the oak tree in the acorn. Rather, we take them out. We did not create the divine presence or the law of good; we commune with this presence and use this law. Therefore, Jesus said that it is God's good pleasure to *give* us the kingdom. It is our business to receive it. And in doing this we follow the same method that any scientist would, for scientists know that they did not create the laws that they use or the principles that they employ.

It is God's good pleasure to give me the kingdom. Today I accept this kingdom, and I accept it in its fullness.

I lay all weariness aside and accept the life-giving, invigorating, dynamic activity of the Spirit, knowing that It vitalizes every organ of my body; It flows with power and strength and purpose through everything I do as It leads me gently down the pathway of life.

Every sense of doubt of any kind is wiped away in the knowledge that today is the day that God has made, and I am made glad in it. Running through me is the silent power of spiritual wisdom and love harmoniously governing my thoughts and actions.

I LEARN
TO LOVE

✤

...perfect love casteth out fear....
I JOHN 4:18

Love is fundamental to life, the great and supreme reality. Love is the highest gift of heaven, the greatest good on earth, and the treasure of all our search. It is the end and aim of everything.

We cannot doubt that God is love, because hate kills while love renews and restores. Love transmits some subtle essence of life to everything it touches, awakening within all things an equal awareness and response. Love is the greatest healing power there is, and no one feels whole without it.

Today my love goes out to all people and all things. There is no fear in this love, for perfect love casts out all fear. There is no doubt in this love, for faith penetrates all doubt and reveals a unity at the center of everything that embraces all things.

This love flowing through me harmonizes everything in my experience, brings joy and gladness to everything, brings a sense of security and well-being to everyone. And I realize that the love flowing through, in, and around me and all things is one vast all-enveloping essence and force forever emanating from the living God. Love alone rules my every experience.

PHYSICAL PERFECTION
IS MINE

And God said, Let us make man in our image....
GENESIS 1:26

When we speak of physical perfection, we are not saying that no one is sick or no one has pain. We are merely implying that of necessity there must be, and is, an essence of perfection at the center of everything, including the physical body. If that which is whole within itself were not already here, neither medicine, psychology, nor affirmative prayer could in any way benefit us physically. Whatever any of these things may do, they cannot create life; they can only reveal it.

Believing as we do in all of the healing arts that help humanity, we do in our practice definitely affirm that toward which they and we all reach—the spiritual center of things.

I now affirm that my body is a body of right ideas. It now is the body of God. Its every action and function is harmonious. Whatever does not belong is eliminated. What needs to be renewed is renewed. All the energy, action, power, and vitality there is in the universe is flowing through this divine creation now.

My word of acceptance does actually establish in my body the action and harmony which already exist. There is one life—perfect, harmonious, whole, complete. That life is my life now—not tomorrow, but today.

I FORGIVE AND
AM FORGIVEN

Judge not, that ye be not judged.
MATTHEW 7:1

It is only when we have completely forgiven others that we can get a clearance in our minds, for we are judged by the judgment with which we judge. If we criticize, condemn, and censure, these are the attitudes that occupy our thinking, and they will not only reflect themselves outwardly, they will also reflect themselves inwardly.

If we want a complete clearance of forgiveness, we must give a complete clearance to everyone and everything. Whether we like it or not, this is one of the great truths of life. Not only should we forgive others, but we should equally forgive ourselves and not carry the mistakes of the past into the future.

Today I affirm that I forgive everyone and am forgiven by everyone. I affirm that the eternal Spirit harbors no malice toward me or anyone else. Forgiving and being forgiven, I have an inward sense of peace and tranquility. There is no anxiety, no sense of guilt, no fear of judgment. All the mistakes of the past are now wiped out of my consciousness, and I am freed of all oppression.

I look forward to the future with joy, in peace and gladness, and live in the present with an inner assurance of being one with life.

I AM RADIANT
WITH HEALTH

…thine health shall spring forth speedily.…
ISAIAH 58:8

Whatever we identify ourselves with, we tend to become. Whatever we think about gradually becomes a subconscious pattern, always tending to manifest itself in our experience. Therefore, we should endeavor to identify our bodies with the spiritual reality which is the very substance and essence of the physical being.

We do not deny the body, but affirm that it is radiant with the perfection of God. There is an inner life of complete perfection at the center of everything; otherwise, nothing could be. We should identify ourselves with this perfect pattern, claiming its reality in our experience.

Today I identify my body with the action of God, the radiant life of the divine being. I identify my physical body with my spiritual body, claiming they are one and the same. I know that every aspect of my body corresponds to the radiant perfection of the living Spirit. There is perfection in every part of my being, perfect wholeness and completeness.

My physical body is a temple of the living Spirit which animates it, sustains it, rebuilds it after the image of Its own perfection, and keeps it in perfect health, harmony, and wholeness.

DIVINE LIFE
ANIMATES ME

Be ye therefore perfect, even as your Father....
MATTHEW 5:48

When Jesus said, "Be ye therefore perfect, even as your Father which is in heaven [within you] is perfect," he was telling us that there is a perfection at the center of all things which, recognized, will spring into being.

We must learn to so identify ourselves with this perfection, so accept it that it is real to us, and so live that it may be expressed through us as what we are. No matter how imperfect the appearance may be, or painful or discordant, there is still an underlying perfection, an inner wholeness, a complete and perfect life, which is God.

I say to my physical body: "Be ye therefore perfect, because you already are perfect in the divine sight. There is one life, that life is God, that life is your life now. This life circulates through you. It animates your whole being. There is no inaction in this divine life. There is no stoppage or hindrance or obstruction to it. Whatever may appear to be to the contrary is transformed and transmuted, for I am identifying you, my physical body, only with the body of pure Spirit."

I now affirm and accept the divine presence as manifesting as my body. There is nothing in me that can deny or reject it. Because God is perfect, I am perfect. And so it is.

GOD LIVES
IN ME

...the Father is in me, and I in him.
JOHN 10:38

All life is one life. Just as every physical substance derives from one universal energy, so there is but one life principle, which is God, in which we all live and from which infinite source our individual lives are drawn. If this life is everywhere present, it is also within us.

To say that the life of God is the only life there is means that our life is not only in God and of God and from God—it *is* God, in and through us. If this were not true, we would have a life separate from God, which would be impossible. We must no longer deny that which we should affirm.

The life of God is my life now. In God, I live and move and have my being, and God lives in me and moves through me.

I deny that there is any life separate from God and affirm that every organ, action, and function of my physical body is animated by the divine life which created and sustains it. It is this life that is circulating through me now with perfect rhythm, revitalizing every function.

I am one with the whole, therefore I say to my mind: "You are to live and think and feel this truth until it is spontaneous and natural. And when you say, 'God is my life,' you are to know that the entire life of the divine presence is flowing through you."

I FIND
NEW VITALITY

✻

...my God shall be my strength.
ISAIAH 49:5

If God is all the life there is, then this life contains
the only energy there is. If we are really hooked up
with the eternal, everlasting, and perfect energy, then
we should never become weary at all. And when we
have an enthusiastic outlook on life, we seldom
become weary. Therefore, we must convince ourselves
that we are vitalized by the strength of God, and we
must do something to ourselves which makes it certain that this infinite energy shall increasingly flow
through us.

It is up to us to make the decision, to follow the
course of affirmative thinking, prayer, and meditation

which shall keep this stream of energy flowing through our minds and bodies.

Today I am energized by the vitality of the living Spirit. All the power that there is, all the energy and vitality that there is, is mine. I am filled with an enthusiasm for living, a joyous expectation of the more that is to be, and a gratitude for what has been and now is.

Every weight or burden of thought or feeling falls away from me as I am now lifted up into the atmosphere of that vitality which knows only the joy of its own being. I now declare that God is my strength.

THE DIVINE
FLOWS THROUGH ME

❧

For as the Father hath life…so hath he given to the Son….
JOHN 5:26

The wise have said that Spirit produces everything, nourishes everything, and maintains everything. It flows through and is in all things, being all that is. There is nothing outside of It. There is a spiritual presence pervading our consciousness, always proclaiming itself to be the source of our being. The enlightened ones of the ages have told us that our recognition of life is God within us recognizing Itself in everything we do.

I know there is one Mind, one Spirit, and one body—the Mind, the Spirit, and the body of God—the universal whole-ness, the ever-present good, the all-sustaining life.

I dismiss and discard all thoughts and feelings which tend to deny this and accept the action of the divine, creative Spirit as now perfectly manifesting in every organ, function, and action of my body. I now become aware that the one Mind is acting through my body in accord with Its own divine perfection, peace, and harmony.

The Divine circulates through me automatically, freely. Every atom of my being is animated by Its action. I know that at all times I have a silent partner walking with me, talking with me, operating through me. I accept this divine flow.

I ACCEPT THE
HEALING OF SPIRIT

It is the spirit that quickeneth....
JOHN 6:63

There is a spiritual body which cannot deteriorate. This spiritual body is already within us. But only as much of it appears as we recognize. Spiritual perfection always responds to our consciousness of it, but it can respond only in such degree as we become aware.

It is because this inward perfection is so insistent that we maintain a physical body. But because we are individuals with volition, we can, as it were, hang a curtain between our physical life and its spiritual cause. Every affirmative statement we make about our body with deep feeling causes the mind to accept Spirit as the substance of the body and tends to heal.

I realize there is a divine presence at the center of my being. I let this recognition flow through my entire consciousness and flow down into the very depths of my being. Every thought and condition contrary to the divine perfection is eliminated. I rejoice in this realization.

I am now made vigorous and whole. I am strong and well. Every breath I draw is a breath of perfection vitalizing, upbuilding, and renewing every cell of my body. I am healed and made whole in the likeness of Spirit. I have complete faith and acceptance that all the statements I have made are now fulfilled as I have believed.

NOW, AM I
MADE WHOLE

🦋

...According to your faith be it unto you.
MATTHEW 9:29

If God is the all-encompassing deity, then our body and every part of it is made out of that which God is. The infinite substance which is of God is the substance of our body; it is constantly flowing through us, taking form in the likeness of perfect, whole, complete cells. There is a perfect pattern for every cell of every organ, every tissue, every bone, and every drop of blood. The cells of the body are filled with life, vitality, strength, and cleanliness as we accept their divine source. And as the body knows no time or degree, it can only respond and express instantaneously.

The divine presence, being everywhere, is present with me. It is that which I really am.

This recognition floods my entire consciousness. I rejoice in my divinity. I am now made vigorous and hardy. I have the stamina of the infinite. I am fortified with God's perfection and right action. I am hale and able-bodied. I now experience the strength and power of the universe.

This breath I now draw, this thought I now establish, fills me with perfection, vitalizing, upbuilding, and renewing every cell of my body this instant. My body now manifests only divine wholeness and perfection.

There is a presence pervading all things:
this presence is God.

There is an intelligence running through all;
this intelligence is God.

There is a power sustaining all;
this power is God.

There is a unity binding all into one perfect whole;
this unity is God.

Relationships and Affairs

I HAVE
CONFIDENCE IN LIFE

❦

Acquaint now thyself with him, and be at peace....
JOB 22:21

As our thought turns to the quietude of our inner-most self, we become conscious of the perfect peace and love and strength of the universal being, the one Spirit. There is refreshment in the realization that this self is all-pervading, in all and through all. It is the source of all life and is everyone's life. There is one great unity of life.

There is but one life, one body of love, and all are part of it—the one being. Every part of nature melts into another in a great transmutation; one part could not exist without the other. In human nature, the fusion of love and thought makes us all one.

In the true meeting of hearts and minds there is scarcely even the need for words. I know that in the one Mind there cannot be misunderstanding; in the one love, all are included. I have absolute faith in the principle of life, the law of love, and so I now permit love to express through me, to radiate from me.

Love transcends all other manifestations. I am filled with confidence that love is a law, and as I embody love and express it, every situation is filled with harmony and every relationship becomes beautiful and worthwhile. Love rules supreme in my life.

GOOD MULTIPLIES
IN MY EXPERIENCE

All things that the Father hath are mine....
JOHN 16:15

We should continually look to the perfect law of liberty, and by following its precepts, we shall be blessed in our deeds. This means that we should keep our eye single or centered on the Spirit which is eternal and embraces all good.

We often wonder why we are so limited, and too frequently place the blame for our limitations upon the will of God. This is only a trick we play upon ourselves in ignorance of the true facts. Limitation is not placed upon us by God, but through our own ignorance of the great freedom that God has bestowed upon us.

I know that I have been given freedom and liberty by my Creator to become a co-creator in my personal affairs. I have been given unlimited freedom to experience, in increasing measure, my true nature which emanates from the Spirit of God within me.

Today I open my consciousness to the divine influx and expect a greater wisdom and guidance and self-expression. I bless everything and know that good multiplies in my experience as I lift up my consciousness to receive it. I turn my thought Godward and accept the wholeness and the abundance and the joy of the eternal Spirit. I daily experience Its perfect fulfillment.

MY ASSOCIATIONS
ARE HARMONIOUS

…by love serve one another.
GALATIANS 5:13

There is one Spirit incarnated in everyone, an immortal presence causing everyone to live. What a difference it would make in our human relationships if we tried to sense the full meaning of the divine incarnation in all people and adjusted our viewpoint to the truth that we are all bound together in the unity of God.

While it may seem to be otherwise, it is still true that behind all this vast array of life there can be but one common cause, one universal Mind, one infinite Spirit flowing into, through, and becoming everything.

I no longer meet people partially, but open my thought and feeling to the truth that there is but one living Spirit in and through all people. The divine presence, with the same impulse of love and life, manifests in infinite variations and is never alike in any two people.

Knowing that the one who loves the most will live the most, today I go forth to meet life as I feel it really is. I shall see only the divine presence in everyone, shall sense and feel the one life in all. I affirm this presence in myself and others and accept its beneficent action. I act as though it were now manifesting as love, therefore I know that it will be, because it already is.

I SEE GOD
IN EVERYONE

...Thou shalt love thy neighbour as thyself.
MATTHEW 22:39

All the great scriptures have announced this transcendent truth: Give, and to you shall be given. Every act carries with it a consequence, bringing the result of the action back to the self. Emerson called it the law of compensation, and Jesus proclaimed the same law, saying that as we sow, so shall we reap.

We also have been admonished not to forget ourselves, but at the same time to remember everyone else. That is, we are to view ourselves each in the other and behold God in all. When we realize love as the great harmony, then we shall all sing the praise of God.

I perceive the action and harmony of God in, back of, and through all things and all people. The Spirit is never separated from any person or event; It unites each to Itself, vitalizing each with the energy of Its own being.

Over all, in all, and through all is the inevitable seed of perfection which proclaims itself in all my relationships as harmony and joy and love. This seed is at the center of my being, and I am an instrument of its perfection. I recognize that I as well as others have a union with God which is perfect and complete and can manifest only as harmonious action.

I PRAY
ARIGHT

...the Father...he doeth the works.
JOHN 14:10

If we feel that our thought, by our will and concentration, must go somewhere and compel things to happen, then we shall put strain into our prayers. This we must avoid. Actually, our thoughts—our prayers—are acted upon by the law of Mind. We do not and could not compel any law to function; we only permit it to act. So it is with the law relating to faith and belief, or affirmative prayer. Something greater than we are is acting.

If we had the same faith in spiritual law that we have in physical laws, then our faith would be complete, and miracles would happen every day just because there is something acting upon our thoughts.

I now turn to the divine center within me, recognizing the presence and the power and the activity of the living Spirit, and affirm that my word is the activity of the law of good. Without effort or strain, but in a relaxed acceptance, I permit this to be so.

I announce that the law of good, governed by divine intelligence, is active in all my affairs. I declare that everything in my life now comes under the control of this intelligence which prospers and harmonizes all things. I affirm that God is creatively active in all my experiences, and I quietly accept the manifestation of my good.

ONLY GOOD
FLOWS FROM ME

…his love is perfected in us.
I JOHN 4:12

Every heart responds to the warmth of love, every mind yearns for its embrace, and no life is complete without it. Love really is the fulfillment of the law of good. Love alone can heal the world and enable people to live together in unity and in peace. Believing that love is the great lodestone of life and that love alone fulfills the law of good, quietly I say to myself:

I believe that God is love. I believe that love is at the center of everything; therefore, I accept love as the healing power of life. I permit love to reach out from me to every person I meet. I believe that love is returned to me from every person I meet.

I trust the guidance of love because I believe it is the power of good in the universe. I feel that love is flowing through me to heal every situation I meet, to help every person I contact. Love opens the way before me and makes it perfect, straight, and glad.

Love converts the commonplace into that which is wonderful; converts weakness into strength, fear into faith. Love is the all-conquering power of Spirit. I walk in confidence with love, which I feel to be everywhere present, within, around, and through me. In that love, I am safe, secure, and cared for.

I ACCEPT THE
ACTION OF GOD

...our sufficiency is of God.
II CORINTHIANS 3:5

We should daily affirm that the divine presence is everywhere, that it is always active in, around, and through us. The infinite power is always active, always dynamic and creative. It is never passive, but is moving in and through everything we do. Just as the one life harmoniously acts in every cell, every organ, and every function of our bodies, so the one Mind moves in and through our every experience.

There is one Mind that governs everything, and I now affirm and accept that this same intelligence now governs my affairs. It is within me and around me at all times, directing, guiding,

*governing, controlling, and leading me happily to the fulfill-
ment of all good purposes. It knows what to do, when to do
it, and how to do it, and I am impelled to act accordingly.*

*I also salute the God-presence in everyone I meet, and I
know that as surely as I do this, the love indwelling them
responds to the same presence within me. We act in the uni-
son of peace and understanding.*

*Recognizing that all of life is the handiwork of God, I
accept Its love and harmony as now manifesting in every
aspect of my experience.*

I SEE GOOD
IN EVERY EVENT

…Be not afraid, only believe.

MARK 5:36

If good is the great reality, while evil is the great
negation or denial of reality, then it follows that we
should see the good in everything and recognize the
apparent evil merely as a theoretical opposite of good.
There is not God and something else. The divine
Spirit inhabits eternity, overshadows everything
including human events, indwells our own soul, and
is released through our own act. Not God, but we
ourselves, are the creators and supporters of moral
evils.

Our vision is beclouded, and the pathway of our
progress is obstructed until we come to know that

God can and does express as good in every person and situation.

I turn to the presence of God at the center of my being, and it is here that I discover the nature of the good which must and does reside in the back of all people and events. It is only normal and natural that good should prevail, and as I realize that this is the nature of God and accept Its manifestation in my life, this is what I experience.

I am resolved to see the good in everyone and every event. I refuse to acknowledge or accept that anything other than good can come into my life. I now face living free of fear and filled with joy.

I ACCEPT
DIVINE GUIDANCE

…God is thy refuge….
DEUTERONOMY 33:27

If God is our creator and our refuge, why is it that we refuse to avail ourselves of this divine security? It appears that we cannot experience the action of God in our lives until we first turn to God, until we embody those things which are of the nature of God.

We cannot experience love while we hate. Neither can we enjoy peace while we remain confused. If we would enjoy harmony in our relationships and affairs, we must first become that harmony which is the very essence of the Divine. This is the seeming mystery of the infinite, invisible essence which surrounds us. It will support us and guide us only as we first turn to it and accept it.

Today I trust in divine guidance. I rely upon God's wisdom to make straight my way, perfecting and harmonizing every situation in my life. My belief is in this divine security, and I know that all is not only well with me and my affairs, but also well with those with whom I associate.

I let my words and acts partake of God's nature, knowing that that which is accepted in my mind is reflected in my life. "Act as though I am, and I will be." The everlasting arms of God support, sustain, and guide me through this day and every day.

I AM IMMERSED
IN PERFECTION

All things were made by him....
JOHN 1:3

If everything good, enduring, and true comes from
God the Creator, then we may be certain that no
matter what the appearance is, the reality is always
perfect. This is why Jesus said we were not to judge
by appearances, but to judge righteously—to let our
knowledge be of the certainty of the divine presence
at the center of everything.

It is this divine presence which we are to recognize through everything. For every apparent situation
or condition that does not reflect the divine perfection, we are to supply a realization of its opposite.
This spiritual awareness transcends and transforms

every difficulty or difficult situation.

Today, knowing that God—good—is alone enduring and true, I recognize that in reality I am a perfect being, living under perfect conditions. I acknowledge negative appearances for what they are, but at the same time affirm that there is no necessity for their continuation.

I acknowledge and declare that the Creator of all things is now manifesting as perfection and harmony in all my experiences. My world is re-created by my inner spiritual awareness of the action of God in my life.

I BLESS
WHAT I HAVE

All things are delivered unto me of my Father....
MATTHEW 11:27

Have you and I the faith to bless that which perhaps seems so very small—a loaf of bread and a fish—and expect it to become multiplied in our experience to such an extent that it would not only bless us but also bless everyone around us? We cannot help but believe that as Jesus broke the bread and blessed it, in his own mind he saw it multiplied and growing and flowing out to those around him.

This is an example we should follow—to bless what we have, recognizing that it flows from a limitless source. We are merely using it and distributing it. There is always more.

Through the act of affirmative prayer, the limitless resources of the Spirit are at my command. The power of the infinite is at my disposal. I now avail myself of the divine bounty and bless everything that I have. I bless everything around me. I bless the events that transpire in my life, everything that goes out, everything that comes in. I acknowledge an increase of good in all I experience.

I bless myself and others, for we are all partakers of the same divine nature. In joy and love, my blessing rests on everything, and the blessing of God rests on me, multiplying the good in my life.

I OVERCOME
ANIMOSITY

🐝

…have peace one with another.

MARK 9:50

There is but one power in the universe, and that power is God. That power manifests in and through all forms, all people, all conditions, and so is at the very center of our being. That power is life itself, and its nature is love—all-good.

Just as the sun's heat warms the atmosphere, so a consciousness of good overcomes every sign of animosity, hate, and disagreement between people, and signs of wrong action in our affairs. Good constitutes the only power, presence, and law, and the knowledge of good overcomes and dissipates everything in opposition to it.

As I now refuse to entertain any thoughts of animosity, I encounter none in my experience. I recognize the power of love and know that good alone is real and enduring. I turn the searchlight of love on every association and every situation, and instantly all inharmony and darkness is dissolved into light. There is complete dissolution of all that opposes the good that flows through me into expression.

Love always protects its own and now makes clear the way before me, eliminating everything that looked like hate and opposition. I am guided into an ever-widening unfoldment of being; my every thought, feeling, and act is an expression of the God-nature—love—through me, and I encounter nothing unlike It.

I EXPERIENCE
SATISFACTION

Thou hast put gladness in my heart....
PSALM 4:7

There is always a power operating through us, a presence inspiring, guiding, and sustaining us. We need to place reliance on this power, in this presence, and feel ourselves to be an outlet of immeasurable good. Because we are in this divine presence, and because it is in us, and because it has all power, we know that our thoughts are made manifest, perfectly demonstrating harmonious relationships and successful action in our affairs.

I know that the creative law of good is infinite and has all power to accomplish. I know its whole desire for me is freedom

and joy. This freedom and joy are satisfactorily and complete-
ly expressed in all my affairs, in all of my relationships.

There is nothing in me that can hinder this expression. I
am conscious that there is an infinite wisdom directing me.
Whatever I should know, I shall know. Whatever I should do,
I shall do. Whatever belongs to me must come to me.

Because infinite intelligence is within me and is mine
now, I am compelled to recognize my greater good; to see more,
to understand and accept and express more. I know the infi-
nite creative law of good is always bringing complete satisfac-
tion into my life.

MY RELATIONSHIPS
ARE GOOD

❧

...we are members one of another.
EPHESIANS 4:25

We need to know that the perfect life of the Spirit is our life and learn to permit It to radiate through our world of thought and action—to express in our experience. When we learn to relax physically and mentally, we can feel flowing through us a vital energy, a dynamic force, a great surge of living power. Then we feel immersed in and saturated by a vital essence of perfection which brings us in tune with life.

Because my whole being is perfect God-life, I have nothing to fear. Every person I meet recognizes the love and peace and wisdom and courage within me. Each person I meet feels our common bond, knows that we are part of the perfect whole, harmonious centers in the great unity of life. No one could wish to harm or hurt me in any way.

I, too, can know only love and understanding for my fellow beings. I know, because I am God in expression, that every circumstance I find myself in is right for me. Because I, as well as those with whom I associate, am an expression of God who is perfect harmony, all my relationships must of necessity be harmonious as I now declare and permit them to be so. God's harmony fills my experience.

I HAVE
GREAT EXPECTATIONS

...with God all things are possible.
MATTHEW 19:26

In spiritual mind treatment, we are dealing with a law as definite as that which takes a cabbage seed and makes a cabbage out of it instead of a cauliflower. We are dealing with a creative principle which acts upon our thinking. This principle we did not create; we may merely use it. It operates upon us like all other forces in nature.

With this in mind, we have every right to expect the unexpected. We should daily affirm that new ideas are coming to us, new ways of doing things; that we are meeting new and wonderful friends, new situations; that joyous things are going to happen to us.

Knowing that there is a creative principle that reacts to that which I entertain in thought, I now establish in my thinking an attitude of expectancy of good things. I let go of the limitations of the past and live with an enthusiastic expectancy of the good that I will encounter today.

I know that nothing is too good to be true and that nothing is too much for the power that can do anything. I expect the unexpected to happen and believe in a greater good than I have yet experienced. I keep my mind open to divine intuition which is the wisdom that guides me.

There is no knowledge that reaches higher ground

Or goes beyond this wisdom you have found,

That love is keeper of the law and all

Who live in love will live in unity

With law; all who obey the law are freed

From pain and failure, loneliness and need.

Peace of Mind and Happiness

LIVING IS
WORTHWHILE

Then shall thy light break forth....
ISAIAH 58:8

When we give a spiritual mind treatment, we are affirming the presence of God in, around, and through us. It is this closeness of the divine presence which gives us the feeling of peace that is accompanied by a consciousness of power.

It is because we do believe this that we can have this feeling, this inner conviction, this sense of certainty which all spiritual teachers have told us is necessary to effective living. There is a power greater than we are. There is a love which casts out all fear. There is a faith which overcomes all obstructions.

I believe that the Spirit within me, which is God, makes perfect and peaceful the way before me. In this faith and knowledge, I discover a great peace of mind, a deep sense of belonging, a complete realization that God is right where I am. I put my whole trust in God and feel an intimate relationship with the presence and power which controls everything.

The Spirit gently leads me, wisely counsels me. I know that the love which envelops everything flows through me to everyone, and with it goes a confidence, a sense of joy and of peace, as well as a buoyant enthusiasm and zest for life. There comes back to me today everything that makes life worthwhile.

RELAXED
LIVING

❦

…let the peace of God rule in your hearts.…
COLOSSIANS 3:15

In a world distraught with so much confusion and chaos, we may wonder if peace really exists anywhere. But we do search for and deeply need an inner abiding sense of calm and tranquility. Peace of mind is what the world is searching after, for without it we have only a sense of insecurity and loneliness.

Without such a peaceful mental attitude there can be no happiness or contentment, no security or confidence. The peace that we seek cannot be found in confusion. But only when the mind is tranquil, like an unruffled body of water, can it reflect the divine images of peace and perfection.

Today I enter into the peace of God. My mind is stilled from all confusion, and I feel a deep and abiding inward relaxation. The Christ Spirit within me, the one child begotten of the only God, is real to me. I keep my mind stayed on this divine inner presence, and letting every thought of discord slip away, I meet the reality of myself, the eternal and changeless truth about me, which is that I am a child of God, I am one with It forevermore.

Here and now, within me, there is a voice that says: "Peace. Be still, and know that I am God." Now is God in me, around me, and through me.

ENLARGED HORIZONS

...now we see through a glass, darkly....
I CORINTHIANS 13:12

How true it is that we do see as through a glass darkly, or only in part. But to all of us there come fleeting moments when our inward vision is opened, and we seem to look out upon a newer and broader horizon. We are all at a certain place in our growth, but there is a complete certainty before us. We shall continuously expand and experience more and more of that life which already is perfect.

There is no reason why this awakening shall not come now. For we are not really waiting on God—God is waiting on us. All nature awaits our recognition, and even the divine Spirit must await our cooperation with It.

Today my eyes are open more widely, and I look out upon a broader horizon. Across all the experiences I may have had which were limited or unpleasant, I now see the rosy hue of a new dawn. Letting go of that which is little, I now enter into a larger concept of life. Dropping all fear, I entertain faith. Realizing that every form of uncertainty is seeing only in part, I open my spiritual eyes to that which is wholeness, which is greater and better.

Today my eyes are open to the breadth and the height and the depth of that life which is God, that life which is good, and that law which is perfect.

A NEW
PERSONALITY

🌿

...For we are also his offspring.
ACTS 17:28

Would it be too much to say that personality is the use or misuse we are making of a unique "something" back of personality which is expressing through it? Would it be too much to say that back of every personality there must be a divine pattern of individualization which personality but dimly perceives and even more inaccurately interprets?

If so, personality has a possibility far beyond anything that is merely physiological or psychological for it has the possibility, not of becoming a mask to hide the reality behind it but, rather, an open countenance through which this individuality shall become expressed.

Today I express myself, believing that there is a presence hidden within me which is both the reality of my true being and the presence of God. I consciously unite my personal self and all its actions with this overdwelling and indwelling reality.

I know that the vitality of the living Spirit flows through my personality, invigorating it. I know that all the warmth and color and beauty that there is is pouring through it. I do not deny my personality, but affirm that all its impulses and actions flow from a greater source, the presence of God in me as what I am.

ELIMINATE
THE NEGATIVE

...be renewed in the spirit of your mind.
EPHESIANS 4:23

Our happiness is not destroyed by the negative experiences through which we have gone, but by our emotional reactions to those experiences carried in the reservoir of our memory. Our experiences are stored in the mind either as happy or disconsolate ones, as life-giving or morbid. Our negative reactions to life, our unhappiness, and perhaps most of our physical disorders, spring from negative emotional reactions which we have buried alive in our memories. Even so, they can have no more reality to us than we permit them to have. Just as yesterday can influence today, today we are creating the possibilities of tomorrow.

Yesterday is gone, tomorrow has not arrived, but today I am living in the eternal present filled with an everlasting good.

There is nothing unhappy or morbid that can remain in my consciousness. I no longer have any fear of yesterday, nor do I anticipate tomorrow with anything other than joyous anticipation.

Only everything that was good in yesterday shall perpetuate itself, and only everything good in today shall create my future. All negative concepts are eliminated from my mind, right now.

TODAY
I LIVE

And God shall wipe away all tears....
REVELATION 21:4

The wisest man who ever lived told us that the knowledge of truth shall make us free. Books of spiritual wisdom have taught us that it is not the one who makes the mistake whom we should seek to destroy; it is the mistake itself which must be erased.

This means that evil has no existence in itself and has no history. No matter what the negations of yesterday may have been, the affirmations of today rise triumphant and transcendent over them. Thus the evils of our yesterdays disappear into their native nothingness. If we persist in seeing the true rather than the false, then that which is true will appear.

Definitely I know that every negative condition of the past is cleared away from my consciousness. I no longer think about it, see it, or believe in it. Nor do I believe that it has any power to influence my present or my future. Yesterday is not, tomorrow is not; but today, bright with hope and filled with promise, is mine.

I cease weeping over the shortcomings and mistakes of yesterday, and, steadfastly beholding the face of divine reality, I resolve to walk in that light wherein there is no darkness. Today I live!

I AM CALM
AND PEACEFUL

🦋

For I am the Lord, I change not....

MALACHI 3:6

All the great scriptures have taught one identical
message—the unity of good. All the sacred
books have been inspired by the one Mind. Each in its
own tongue has told the story of reality. "...I am the
Lord, I change not...." God is in Itself, by Itself, full
and perfect.

If we can add to this glorified concept the realization that this divine being is the breath of our breath,
omnipresent, forever within us, then we shall realize
that we live in the eternal and perfect Mind. This
means that while we live in the eternal God who does
not change, we are forever drawing from It the possi-

bility of manifold expressions which make living interesting.

I know that the changeless abides within me. I am calm and peaceful in the midst of confusion. I know that nothing disturbs the soul. Peace, infinite peace, is at the center of my being.

I live, move, and have my being in that which is perfect, complete within itself. That self is my self. There is continual, interesting variety in my experience, but it bows from and is an expression of life at the center of my being, which is always harmonious in its action.

I BESTOW THE
ESSENCE OF LOVE

...love is the fulfilling of the law.
ROMANS 13:10

Love is the fulfillment of the law; that is, we never can make the most perfect use of the law unless that use is motivated by love, by a sincere desire to express unity, harmony, and peace.

As true artists wed themselves to the essence of beauty, imbibing its spirit that they may transmit it to the canvas, so we must wed ourselves to the essence of love, that we may imbibe it and, transmitting it, give loveliness to all events. We should not hesitate to express our appreciation for people, things, and events. There is too little enthusiasm about life.

I now rejoice in living. All my sorrows, unhappiness, and regrets are definitely and quietly subjected to the transmuting quality of love. Divine love never remains abstract, but in a vital and dynamic manner molds every aspect of my experience.

As I accept the action of love in my life, I bestow the essence of love upon everything. This love is a healing power touching everything into wholeness, healing the wounds of experience with its balm. With enthusiasm and joy, I embody love in my thoughts and acts, and the perfect action of the law makes love manifest in my experience. Everything is beautiful and meaningful as I accept and express love in every way.

I LIVE IN
CHANGELESS REALITY

Beloved, now are we the sons of God....
I JOHN 3:2

Neither the will of God nor the nature of God can change. Reality is the same yesterday, today, and tomorrow. Everyone's real nature is spiritual, is of God. The only thing about it that can change is that which ought not to be permanent.

Though the real self is changeless, we live in a changing world. It is wonderful to know that something permanent, substantial, and eternal stands in the midst of our being and, I believe, watches with joy the eternal unfoldment taking place. To the Spirit, changes are merely variations of experience.

The Spirit is never caught, bound, or tied, and I, being an expression of Spirit, am never limited by the world of experience. Negative experiences may seem to exist for a brief moment, but beauty, like truth, exists forever. All unlike God in my life ceases to exist when confronted with the divine reality of my being.

I live in a changeless reality. I am not disturbed by the passage of time or the variations of experience which I go through. The Divine acting in, through, and around me is changeless in Its manifestation of good, and I rest secure in the knowledge that as changes occur in my life, they are always changes for the better. My good alone endures.

MY HEART SINGS

...thou shalt make me full of joy....
ACTS 2:28

Emerson says that prayer is the proclamation of a joyful and a beholding soul. The Bible makes many references to the joy of God and the gladness that we should have in God's presence.

How can we help but be glad and filled with joy when we believe that the presence and power that is back of everything is one perfect life, forever giving of itself, forever imparting itself to us, forever flowing through us in wondrous light and power. All nature is alive, awake, and aware with the divine presence, and everything in life responds to the song of the heart.

Today I am filled with joy. I let every sense of depression or heaviness depart from my mind and let my soul be lifted up in song to the giver of all life and to the joy of living. Joy is my companion, happiness my comrade. There is a song in my heart singing unto the Creator of all things, and there is an invisible chorus responding through everything in nature and every person I meet.

I proclaim this day to be one of happiness, of thanksgiving and praise to the most high God, to the divine presence that inhabits eternity and has a dwelling place in my own soul. I express joy and gratitude to this inner presence—my Almighty God in my heaven.

I GUARD
MY THOUGHTS

...be not consumed one of another....

Here we find the law of cause and effect. In the long run, if we seek to harm another, we find that we are only harming ourselves. The spiritually wise have always taught that our thoughts ride on a return circuit and that they never fail to react upon us. Until we have transcended any negative causation we have set in motion, we shall suffer.

This is why we should do to others what we would like them to do to us. In this law alone can we find exact justice. The universal imposes neither evil nor limitation upon us. However, being free agents, we may and must experience, at least temporarily, the result of our own negative thoughts and acts.

Today I shall guard all of my thoughts, seeing to it that nothing emanates from my consciousness other than that which blesses, builds, and heals. I shall not worry about the consequences, for they already exist in the mathematical law of cause and effect. This law does not govern me; it is something which I govern. If nothing goes forth from me which can hurt, then nothing can return to me which can harm.

The knowledge of this makes me wise. Faith in the justice of the universal is my altar. On it I lay my offering—thoughts of peace, of joy, and of prosperity.

LOVE
SURROUNDS ME

...If we love one another, God dwelleth in us....
I JOHN 4:12

When we let the love that is within us go out to the God who is in all people and the divine presence that is in all things, then we are loving God with all our heart and with all our soul and mind—we are recognizing that the Spirit within us is the same Spirit that we meet in others. This is loving our neighbors as ourselves. When we recognize the divine presence everywhere, then we know that it responds to us and that there is a law of good, a law of love, forever giving of itself to us.

This divine and perfect law is circulating through me right now. Its rhythm is in my heartbeat; its perfection is manifest in every organ, action, and function of my physical body.

Love and perfect life circulate through everything. This love and this life I accept as the truth about myself, now and forever. The law of love heals and makes whole, makes me prosperous and happy. I know that the only power there is and the only presence there is, is love, the Spirit Almighty.

There is no condemnation, no judgment, and no fear in me. I feel that I belong to the world in which I live; I love people and am loved of them. I feel secure in life.

HAPPINESS
IS MINE

...there are pleasures for evermore.
PSALM 16:11

Nothing in our thought about God should produce sadness or depression; rather, it should do quite the reverse, because our faith in and love of God should give us such a confidence and such a sense of security that we should indeed be able to say: "Joy to the world, the Lord has come."

We need to come to realize that God is not in some far-off place, but instead that God is an inward intimate presence closer to us than our very breath. God cannot separate Itself from us, but too often we separate ourselves from God.

I now affirm that there is nothing in me that can doubt this presence or limit the power of good in my life. There is nothing in me that can separate me from the love of God, and I accept the joy of living in the very midst of it. The divine presence leads me on the pathway of peace. It directs my thoughts, my words, and my actions into constructive channels of self-expression. It unites me with others in love, in kindness, and in consideration.

Today I accept this action gratefully and realize that it brings into my experience everything necessary to my happiness. I affirm for others that which I accept for myself, for good cannot belong to me alone.

I RECOGNIZE
MY DIVINITY

The spirit of God hath made me....

JOB 33:4

Each person is a spirit, but we seldom recognize this greatest of all truths about ourselves. Seldom do we consciously invite communion with the Spirit or open all the doorways of our thought in complete awareness.

The Bible tells us to let that mind be in us which was in Jesus, which is of course the Mind of God and the invisible guest in every person. There is always available within us that which can wisely counsel, unerringly lead, and direct our thoughts and actions in harmony, peace, and cooperation.

I know there is a presence that came with me when I entered this life, and I know that this same presence will go with me when I leave this physical form, for it is the presence of eternal life, the life that cannot die. And because God cannot fail, and because the divine presence within me is God as my real self, I know that there is a power flowing through my word of faith which makes straight the way before me.

I now have no fear of the past, the present, or the future, and today I am living in the knowledge that God is over all and through all. I feel this presence as perfection, love, and goodness making my life whole and complete.

THE GLADNESS OF LIVING

...we are the children of God.

Romans 8:16

Affirmative prayer means that we clear the mind of all doubt and fear and turn in faith to the great giver of life. It means that we become aware of the presence of God within and around us, here and now. It means that we affirm this presence and accept it quietly, calmly, and peacefully, in all of its fullness. We let go of every anxious thought; surrender every doubt and fear. We look out upon the world and say that it is our world, and it is a good world because it is God's world.

In this knowledge, we receive confidence and inspiration from the source of all life, and divine love guides our every action.

I now accept the domain which God has given. I accept the life which Spirit has implanted within me, and this life reaches out to everything around me in joy and gladness and with the blessed assurance that all is well.

I affirm that there is nothing that can hinder me from entering into the fullness and completeness of my own self-expression and perfection of being. In this I have a faith, a conviction, an assurance that cannot be moved, for as a child of God I am established in and surrounded by God's Love. Only joy, happiness, and gladness fill all the days of my life.

THE FULL LIFE

Herein is my Father glorified, that ye bear much fruit....
JOHN 15:8

God could not withhold Itself from me. That which It is, It has given fully unto me to enjoy. The life of God is perfect, it is eternal, it is the essence of all things. That life is God's gift to me. Therefore this fullness is within me, ready to manifest through me as I partake of it. Even though I am divinely endowed, I partake of my divinity only as I let it be embodied.

I now consciously begin to draw upon the life which is mine. I now begin to definitely re-educate myself in the belief that there is given unto me a fullness of life to experience, which is divine in its origin, eternal in its presence, and always fully available. I now accept that the life of the Spirit is my life.

The infinite richness of the Spirit is mine to enjoy. The vital good health, the wisdom, the peace, and all the good things which proceed from the Spirit, I now claim. The act of accepting them is my right and privilege, and I exercise it intelligently and in full faith.

Life now sings through me in radiant ecstasy.

SCIENCE OF MIND
It Will Change Your Life

Recognized as one of the foremost spiritual teachers of this century, Ernest Holmes blended the best of eastern and western spiritual philosophies, psychology, and science into the transformational ideas known as the Science of Mind. Additionally, he formulated a specific type of meditative prayer, known as spiritual mind treatment, which has positively changed the lives of millions.

Basing his techniques for living a free and full life on sacred wisdom, from the ancient to the modern, Ernest Holmes outlines these ideas in a collection of inspiring books. Written with simplicity and clarity, these books provide the means for every reader to live a more satisfying life.

For a list of books by Ernest Holmes, call 1-800-382-6121.

The award-winning *Science of Mind* magazine presents insightful and uplifting articles, interviews, and features each month. Each issue's *Daily Guides to Richer Living* provide you with spiritual wisdom and inspiration for every day of the month.

For more information, call 1–800–247–6463.

SCIENCE OF MIND
A philosophy, a faith, a way of life
Science of Mind Publishing
2600 West Magnolia Boulevard
Burbank, CA 91505

*Visit Science of Mind on-line at
www.scienceofmind.com.*